It Starts with food Recipes.
For your Nutritional Reset
by Laura Hill

Disclaimer:

The information provided in this book is designed to provide helpful information on the subjects discussed. The publisher and author are not responsible for any specific health or allergy needs that may require medical supervision and are not liable for any damages or negative consequences from any treatment, action, application or preparation, to any person reading or following the information in this book.

Table of Contents

I want to Thank and Congratulate you for Buying this Book "It Starts with food Recipes: Delicious and Healthy Paleo Recipes For your Nutritional Reset' *You are about to discover proven techniques to lose weight by changing the foods you eat for the next 30 Days, With this great book in your Palms you would start seeing changes in No Time, because this Diet Program is Proven to Work.*

In the world that we are living, we all need to step back and think about all the unhealthy things that we are putting into our bodies. We are unhealthy, overweight and even unfit. The Whole30 program is the program that will get back a healthy body, which is fit and slim.

What is the Whole30 program?

The Whole30 program is all about eating healthy and stops those cravings for all the sugar and unhealthy foods that we are putting in our bodies. And, it will restore your metabolism. This diet was founded by Dallas and Melissa Hartwig in 2009. And since then many people has benefited from this program by being healthier.

With this program you will learn which foods are having a negative impact to your body and which foods are good for your body. Even, if we know that too much sugar is bad for us, we still don't know how to stay away from it. In the 30 days that you are on the program, you will learn what foods to eat, and what foods to avoid sustaining a healthy and fit body.

By going on this program you will have many benefits. Even, if you have some health issues. With this program you will feel and look better in just 30 days.

You need to know what kind of foods you may eat when you are on the Whole30 program. There are more foods that you can eat than you think. When you read all the foods that you can't eat, you will maybe wonder if there are any foods still left that you can eat. However, these foods are the foods that you are allowed to eat while on the program.

Vegetables:

We all know that vegetables are good for you. But, with this program vegetable is very important. When you are buying your vegetables, you must try to buy only organic vegetables. Some of the vegetables that you can eat are: Acorn Squash, beets, bell peppers, garlic, carrots, kale, greens, onions, tomato, Zucchini, etc. The more vegetables you eat, the better. Don't throw any sugar or butter on the vegetables when you are cooking them.

Fruits:

Just like the vegetables, you must try to buy these fruit organic. Then you will know that you are eating as natural as possible. The fruits that are best to eat on this program are definitely apricots, blackberries, cherries, grapefruit, kiwi, melon, plum, raspberries and strawberries. You can eat the other fruits as well, but these are the best that you can eat during the 30 days.

Fats that you can use:

We all know that when you are preparing food, you need to use some sort of fat to prepare the food, especially if you want to have tastier foods. But, therefor you need to know what fats are the best to use. You can't use just any fat for preparing your dishes. These fats are safe to use; Animal fats, clarified butter, ghee, avocado fats, coconut butter, olive oil and other olive products, coconut oil and coconut milk. You should not try to use other types of fats for preparing your food.

Seafood:

Most people that are on this program are glad that seafood is allowed. Seafood is healthier than most of us thinks. The secret with seafood is the way you are preparing them. You can use garlic, but you must be careful of the fat that you are adding to the seafood. The best type of seafood to eat is wild- caught and sustainably fished seafood. This seafood is the best.

- *Red meats:*

When you are on the Whole30 program, you don't need to avoid red meat. There are many diets that don't allow you to eat any form or red meat. However, if you are eating red meat, you need to find organic meat. This red meat is ideal to eat when you are on this diet: beef, buffalo, lamp, elk, venison, etc. You just need to remember that the lean, fat-free meat is the best to buy.

- *Poultry:*

Lean poultry or fat-free poultry is also allowed with this program. The poultry that is included in this diet is organic; chicken, turkey, duck and pheasant. If you can't find organic poultry you just need to be aware of removing any fat or skin of these poultry. Then you will be able to eat it during the 30 days.

- *Non-ruminants:*

Most of the non-ruminants has a lot of fat and can be quite unhealthy. But, if you are making sure that they are organic of lean, then it shouldn't be a problem. Examples of organic non-ruminants that you can eat are; pork, wild boar, rabbit, etc. The products that are made from these animals can also be eaten, but again make sure that it is lean products and the organic products are still the best. Here we are talking about bacon and sausages. And, make sure about the labels for forbidden ingredients.

Eggs:

Also some diets are forbidding eggs, but eggs are allowed on the Whole30 program. You should look for the organic or pastured eggs, if you want to include eggs into your new diet. You just need to be careful in what fat you are preparing your eggs, and what ingredients you are adding to your eggs. All the ingredients should still be the ones that you are allowed to eat.

We have prepared for you delicious Paleo/ Whole 30 Recipes to help you stick to the whole 30 Program, so you don't go out of food ideas. Enjoy this Delicious and Healthy Meal while you lose that Extra Pounds.

Now on to the Recipes...

There is no doubt that breakfast is the most important meal of the day. It is important that you make time to eat the best and not gobble up or starve yourself. Here are Mouthwatering and healthy Breakfast recipes that are quick to make and great to help you get rid of all those extra fat.

Omelet with Fruits

If you have a busy day schedule, and you do not have enough time to make heavy breakfast, try this simple and tasty omelet. It will take you only few to prepare this meal, and it will give you enough energy for the whole day to be fresh and active.

Yields: 2 Servings

What you need:

4 Eggs
Bacon (According to your taste)
Fruits (banana and strawberries) Sliced (as per your taste)
Sea salt or Pepper (As per taste)
1 teaspoon Oil

How You make it:

1. Warm up a frying pan and add a few drops of oil in it.
2. Pour the beaten eggs in the pan and wait till it start to bubble.
3. As soon as the bubbles start to appear and eggs begin to solidify, add bacon to it. Flip one side of the omelet to the other.
4. Let the omelet cook for a few minutes, or until the edges of the eggs become brown.
5. Sprinkle salt or pepper over it, as per your taste.
6. Serve the delicious omelet with sliced strawberries and bananas.

Whole 30 Scrambled Eggs

Scrambled eggs are a great way to start your day. Here is a yummy recipe for your famished stomachs.

Yield: 2 Servings

What you need:

3 eggs

1 cup sliced onions

½ cup tomatoes

1 Tablespoon Olive Oil

1 Tablespoon pine nuts

Salt and pepper, to taste

How you make it:
In a frying pan, pour in the olive oil and add in the onions and cook till golden brown. Add in the tomatoes and fry for 5 minutes.

Remove the mixture from flame and set it aside.

In a bowl, whisk the eggs well, add salt and pepper according to your taste. Next add in the onion and tomatoes into the egg mixture.

Now cook the egg mixture on low flame and stir continuously until it is scrambled well. Add in the pine nuts.

Remove from heat and serve.

Paleo Porridge

This is a great warm and sweet porridge recipe to start your day. It is a great breakfast option and takes just a few minutes to make.

Yield: 2 Servings

What you need:

½ cup almonds

1 Teaspoon raw honey

¾ cup coconut cream

1 Teaspoon cinnamon powder

Dash of cloves

Dash of nutmeg

Dash of cardamom

How you make it:

1.   In a saucepan, heat the coconut cream till it becomes liquid.

2.   Ground the almonds using a blender or food processor and add the honey to it. Blend it well.

3.   Add the almond mixture into the saucepan. Keep stirring for 5 minutes till it becomes thick.

4.   Lastly sprinkle the nutmeg, cardamom, and cloves.

Porridge with Coconut Milk

We all know that porridge is one of the best things to have breakfast with. It is tasty and nutritious at the same time. Here we are sharing a delicious recipe of Paleo porridge with coconut milk.

Yields: 2-4 Servings

What you need:

2 fresh Bananas (ripen and mashed)
2 cups Coconut milk (you can also take one can, but will have to use some water as well)
¼ cup Flax
1 tsp Cinnamon
1/8 tsp Nutmeg (ground)
Sea salt to taste (or 1/8 teaspoon)
½ tsp Ginger
Maple syrup (Optional)
1/8 tsp (ground) Cloves
Honey (Optional)
¾ cup of Almond meal
Berries, nuts, seeds, or coconut flakes to be used as topping

How to make it:

1. Add all the ingredients in a pan and let it cook on low flame.
2. Keep it stirring, unless the mixture starts to get thicken.
3. The consistency of the mixture solely depends on the coconut milk you use.
4. It may look thinner at first, but get thicken quickly, even after serving.
5. You may have to add some water or more coconut milk in it.

Banana Bread

Here is a Paleo Banana Bread recipe that you can make without using the standard ingredients. Enjoy every last bite without any guilt!

Yield: 3 Servings

What you need:

¼ cup raw honey

3 eggs, separated

¼ cup olive oil

2 mashed bananas

1 Teaspoon 100% vanilla essence

1½ cups almond meal

How you make it:

1.   Pre-heat your oven to 180 degrees Celsius.

2.   In a bowl, beat the egg yolks till it is light and fluffy. Blend in the honey.

3.   Next add in the olive oil, bananas and vanilla essence.

4.   To this mixture add in the ground almond meal and stir well.

5.   In another bowl, beat the egg whites till they form stiff peaks.

6.   Fold this in the banana mixture.

7.   Line the mold with baking paper and pour this batter into the mold.

8.   Cook in oven for 30 minutes at 180 degrees Celsius.

Here is a classic eggs and bacon Whole 30 recipe.

Yields: 3 Servings

What you need:

115grams bacon meat

8 egg whites

Pepper and salt, to taste

1 onion

1 Tablespoon Olive oil

How you make it:

1.   In a frying pan, pour in the olive oil.

2.   Cook the bacon on a medium flame.

3.   Chop the onions finely and add it in the frying pan. Keep stirring until it turns brown.

4.   When the onions and bacon are cooked, add in the egg whites and scramble it altogether.

5.   Sprinkle with pepper and salt and serve with lettuce.

Nutty Energy Bar

Here is a healthy nutty and nutritious energy bar recipe *that is* convenient and can be eaten on-the-go.

What you need:

½ cup pecan nuts

¼ cup coconut oil

¼ cup coconut

¼ cup hazelnut butter

¼ cup almond butter

1 ½ Teaspoon vanilla extract

1 egg

Salt

½ cup dried blueberries

How you make it:

1. In a bowl, melt the hazelnut butter and coconut oil until it forms a smooth paste.

2. To this mixture add in the vanilla extract and salt.

3. In a separate bowl, shred the coconut until is fine.

4. On a tray, toast the pecan nuts and coconut until it is golden brown.

5. When it is toasted, blend it till it is a coarse powder. Blend this in with the butter mixture.

6. Add in the egg and mix well, and fold in the blueberries.

7. Press this mixture in a loaf pan and cook at 325 degrees for around 10 minutes.

8. Allow it to cool and cut into smaller pieces.

9. You can store it in an airtight container.

Casseroles are a great breakfast option that can be stored for a few days. This breakfast casserole recipe is something that your whole family can enjoy.

Yields: 4 Servings

What you need:

1 small onion

Pork sausage

1 cup spinach

2 Tablespoons olive oil

1 sweet potato

5 eggs

½ cup coconut milk

Dash of nutmeg

Salt and pepper, to taste

How you make it:

1. Preheat the oven to 400 degrees Fahrenheit.

2. Peel and cut sweet potatoes into small pieces. Add in the olive oil, salt and pepper and roast them in oven for 15 minutes.

3. Cut and sauté your onions in olive oil till the onions are caramelized.

4. Next cook the sausage on medium heat.

5. In a separate bowl, whisk the eggs, coconut milk, nutmeg, salt, and pepper. Blend it well.

6. In a baking dish, assemble the browned sausage at the bottom followed by the caramelized onions and roasted potatoes. Top it with the spinach.

7. Next pour in the egg and coconut mixture to cover all the ingredients.

8. Bake at 350 degrees Fahrenheit for 20-30 minutes.

Zucchini Meat Balls

Zucchini is a great vegetable to add to your whole 30 diet. Here is a quick recipe for you.

Yields: 4 Servings

What you need:

300 grams beef

300 grams grated zucchini

2 eggs

1 onion

1 cup almond meal

1 Teaspoon salt

½ Teaspoon Pepper

How you make it:

1. In a mixing bowl, add in the beef and zucchini.

2. Next blend in the eggs and combine it well.

3. Chop the onions well and add in the almond meal.

4. Roll the mixture into little balls.

5. Line your tray with the baking paper and place it in the oven.

6. Pre-heat the oven to 180 degrees Celsius.

7. Bake it for 30 minutes at the same temperature.

Potato And Carrot Fritters

These potato and carrot fritters are easy to make and easier to devour. Plus it gives you all the proteins you need!

Yield: **4 Servings**

What you need:

2/3 cup grated potato

½ cup grated carrot

½ cup chopped almonds

2 eggs

Salt and pepper, to taste

Coconut oil

What you need:

1. In a mixing bowl, add in the potatoes.

2. To this you need to add in the grated carrots.

3. Next whisk the eggs well and add in the eggs.

4. Combine the almonds and salt and pepper.

5. Mix all the ingredients well and make small patties.

6. In a frying pan, heat the coconut oil on medium flame and cook the patties on both sides for 5 minutes or until it is well cooked.

Breakfast Waffles

Yield 2 servings

What you need:

2 bananas
4 organic eggs, beaten
2 tablespoons coconut oil
1 cup almond milk
½ cup almond flour
¼ cup natural shredded coconut
1/3 tablespoon cinnamon
Salt, just a pinch

How you make it:

1. Preheat the waffle iron.
2. In a bowl, blend bananas, coconut oil, almond milk and eggs.
3. In a separate bowl, add in the almond flour, salt, shredded coconut and cinnamon.
4. Combine ingredients of both bowls. Mix well.
5. Once the batter is formed, pour the mixture into the waffles iron and cook until done.
6. Serve and enjoy.

Yield: 3 Servings

What you need:

3 organic eggs
3 large steaks
4 tablespoons olive oil
Salt to taste
Black pepper to the taste
Paprika to the taste
1 teaspoon of ginger garlic paste

How you make it:

1. First, season the steak with salt, pepper, paprika, and ginger garlic paste and Let it sit for 10 minutes.
2. In a frying pan, heat oil over low to medium flame.
3. Cook the steak for about 4 minutes per side.
4. Place the steak in separate serving plate.
5. Add a bit more oil and fry the egg in the same pan.
6. Serve over steak and enjoy.

Walnut and Berry Pancake

Yield: 2 servings

What you need:

3 cups of almond flour
Pinch of salt
2 organic eggs
3 teaspoons of walnut oil
½ cup of chopped walnuts
½ cup of blueberries
1 teaspoon of baking powder
Honey (optional)

How you make it:

1. In a medium bowl, add almond flour, baking powder, salt and chopped walnuts.
2. In a separate small bowl, beat eggs and add walnut oil.
3. Combine ingredients of both bowl and then fold blueberries at the end.
4. Pour the spoon full of the mixture into the cooking pan to make the pancakes.
5. Once the top gets bubbly flipped to cook from the other side.
6. Once the pancake cooked thoroughly, serve with the drizzle of honey on top.

Eggplant Balls

Yield: 4 Servings

What you need:

2 medium onions, diced
4 medium eggplants, diced
2-3 tablespoons water
2 tablespoons walnuts, toasted and chopped
½ teaspoon salt
4 cloves garlic, minced
4 tablespoons olive oil
2 lemons, zests
6 large eggs

How you make it:

1. Preheat oven at 370 degree F.
2. Take a cooking pan and heat oil, then sauté onions for 5 minutes.
3. Add in eggplant and 3 tablespoons water, and cook for 15 minutes with the lid on.
4. Sprinkle salt and add walnuts.
5. Once the eggplants get soften, add walnuts.
6. After cooking for 5 more minutes, turn off the heat and let the mixture cool.
7. Next, puree the mixture in blender and then add all the remaining ingredients
8. Make the ball of eggplant mixture with hand and bake in preheated oven for about 15 minutes.
9. Serve and enjoy.

This can be a pleasant springtime breakfast with the freshness of asparagus and the flavors of leeks, garlic and chives. Even though I have used bacon in the recipe, any breakfast meat of your choice can be used. Soak in the early sunshine while having this delicious breakfast!

Yield: 4 Servings

What you need:

· 4 eggs

· 4 slices of bacon

· 1 sliced leek

· 1 bunch of asparagus

· 1 clove of minced garlic

· 2-3 tablespoons fresh chimes, minced

· Sea salt and freshly ground pepper

How you make it:

1. Pre heat your oven to 400 F.

2. Place a skillet over medium heat and cook the bacon for about 3 minutes per side.

3. Add the garlic and leek and cook for 2-3 minutes.

4. Add the asparagus and cook until tender.

5. Add the eggs to the skillet.

6. Add the seasoning and place in the oven for 2-3 minutes. Garnish with fresh chives.

Sweet potatoes can be eaten in moderation in a paleo diet .They do not contain the anti-nutrients that potatoes contain. This recipe is nutritious and makes an extremely delectable breakfast dish.

Yield: 2 Servings

What you need:

- 2 eggs
- 1 sweet potato diced into small cubes
- 2 Tablespoons coconut oil, divided into 2 parts
- ½ yellow onion, diced
- 1 bell pepper, diced
- 2 nitrate free sausages, sliced
- Black pepper, freshly ground

How you make it:

1. Take a skillet and pour the coconut oil into it.
2. Heat it in medium heat.
3. Add the sweet potatoes and onion and sauté it for 5 minutes. Now, add the sausages and cook it until the sausages turn brown.
4. Add bell pepper and a tablespoon of water. Cover and cook for 15 min.
5. Take a pan and fry the eggs in the remaining coconut oil.
6. Season it with ground pepper and top it over the sweet potato hash and serve

Tasty Almond Banana Pancakes

Who can resist the lure of pancakes for breakfast?

Almonds contain Vitamin E, B Vitamins, essential minerals and healthy fan. It is good for the heart and the brain. Bananas are very nutritive and considered to be one of the healthiest foods in the world. This diet combines the goodness of these two super foods.

Yield: 2 servings

What you need:

- 2 bananas
- 2 Tablespoons almond butter
- 2 eggs
- Fresh blueberries
- 1 tablespoon coconut flour
- ¼ cup of almonds and walnuts

How you make it:

1. Take a bowl and mash the bananas in it.

2. Add all the other ingredients and whisk well, until it forms a consistent mixture.

3. Grease a skillet with coconut oil and heat it to medium.

4. Pour the batter into the skillet and to form circles 3-4 inches in diameter.

5. Flip it when ready and cook the other side.

6. Make sure that the skillet is well greases after each round of pancakes.

This is a healthy variation of the traditional apple pie. We bake the pies inside the apple and not in some nut-flour crust. The vanilla and cinnamon give it a sweet and classy taste. The walnuts make it crunchy and healthy. You can pamper your sweet tooth while sticking to healthy eating.

Yield: 4 Servings

What you need:

large apples

¼ cup chopped walnuts

½ teaspoon pure vanilla extract

½ teaspoon ground cinnamon

Tablespoon raw honey

How you make it:

1. Preheat your oven to 275F.

2. Take 4 apples and cut off the tops and keep it aside to be used later.

3. Scoop out the inside of each apple very carefully, with a spoon.

4. Do not break the peel.

5. Take the remaining 2 apples and cut them into thin slices after peeling the skin.

6. Transfer the sliced apples to a bowl and add the cinnamon, vanilla, walnuts and honey and mix well.

7. Scoop this mixture into the hollow apples and cover each apple with the top.

8. Take a roasting pan and place the stuffed apples in it.

9. Pour some water to cover the bottom.

10. Cover this pan with a foil and bake for 20 minutes.

11. Now, remove the foil and bake for another 15 to 200 minutes.

12. Your healthy, Paleo apple pie is ready!

If quiche is something you love, you will be happy to know it is a great Paleo meal. Since it mainly uses egg it is a great start to your morning.

Yields: 4 Servings

Requirements for Zucchini Crust:
2 zucchini

11/2 Tablespoon coconut flour

1 Tablespoon coconut oil

1 egg

Salt to taste

Method for Crust:
1. Preheat the oven to 400 degrees Fahrenheit, and grease the pie dish.
2. Grate the zucchini and wrap it in cheesecloth, and drain the zucchini.
3. Add in the coconut flour, egg and coconut oil and mix it together.
4. Place this mixture into the pie dish and spread it around.
5. Bake it for 10 minutes and set it aside.

Requirement for Quiche:
2 cups ham

2 cups broccoli

2 cups onions

8 eggs

1 Teaspoon coconut oil

3 Tablespoons water

Salt and pepper, to taste

Method for Quiche:

1. Chop the broccoli and steam it lightly for 5 minutes.

2. In a pan, pour in the coconut oil and sauté the ham and onions.

3. In a mixing bowl, blend in the eggs, water and spices and the ham mixture.

4. Pour the entire mixture on the zucchini crust and place broccoli on top.

5. Bake for 25 – 30 minutes. Let it cool for a while before slicing it.

It may not be easy to squeeze in a meal at lunch if you are working or busy, but it is very necessary for your health and yes for your sanity too! Making time for your midday meal will reenergize you and keep you active. Here are Healthy and Delicious Whole 30 lunch recipes that are tasty and yes will help you lose weight too!

Asparagus, beef, parsley and other healthy ingredients combine to make this delicious main course.

Yields: 2 Servings

What you need:

1 onion
1/2 bunch green or white asparagus,
2 red bell peppers
1 garlic clove
4 beef pieces
1 Tablespoon ginger
Parsley
Coconut oil
Salt and pepper to taste

What you need:

1. Finely chop the onion, red peppers, asparagus, and ginger.
2. Stir-fry the vegetables one by one and set aside.
3. In a wok, add in some coconut oil to stir-fry the beef strips and cook over high heat.
4. To this add in the garlic and onion.
5. Next add in the asparagus and bell peppers and stir fry for another few minutes.
6. Finally season it with the ginger, salt and pepper.
7. Garnish it with parsley.

Shrimp Fried Rice Recipe

Yields: 2 Serving

What you need:

1 yellow onion, chopped
2 cup shrimps
2 heads of cauliflower
2 organic eggs
2 cloves of garlic
4 tablespoons olive oil
Salt and pepper to taste

How you make it:

1. Chop cauliflower in a food processor.
2. Next, heat oil in frying pan and sauté onions and garlic.
3. Add the cauliflowers and cook until soften.
4. Add shrimp to skillet and cook for additional 10 minutes.
5. Beat egg in a bowl and sprinkle pepper and salt.
6. Pour the egg into shrimp mixture and cook until eggs fluffy.
7. Serve and enjoy.

Paleo Zucchini Patties

Yield: 4 servings

What you need:

4 zucchinis
4 green onions
5 organic eggs
Salt and pepper to taste
3-5 tablespoons of olive oil

How you make it:

1. First, wash the zucchinis and then grate it with the cheese grater.
2. In a small bowl, combine zucchini, eggs, green onions, salt and pepper.
3. Make patties with hand.
4. Next, take a skillet and heat oil in it.
5. Fry the patties in skillet.
6. Once the both sides cooked thoroughly serve and enjoy

Paleo Chicken Tortilla Soup

This one is from the Mexican kitchen. It is a gluten free, dairy free, low carb, low fat variation of the traditional chicken tortilla soup. This is a wonderfully healthy recipe that completely adheres to the paleo philosophy.

Yield: 6 servings

What you need:

- 2 large chicken breasts, skinned and cut into small, ½ inch strips
- 1 can (28 oz) of diced tomatoes
- 1 diced sweet onion
- 2 Cups of shredded carrots
- 32 ounces organic chicken broth
- 2 jalapenos de-seeded and diced
- 4 Cloves of minced garlic
- 2 Cups of chopped celery
- 1 bunch of chopped cilantro
- 1 Teaspoon chilli powder
- 1 Teaspoon cumin
- 2 Tablespoons Tomato paste
- Olive oil
- Sea salt and freshly ground pepper
- 2 Cups of water

How you make it:

1. Place a Crockpot over medium heat and add a dash of olive oil.

2. Add the chicken broth to it .Add onion, garlic, jalapeno, salt and pepper and cook until it becomes soft.

3. Now, add the remaining ingredients and cover and cook for 2 hours.

4. Add salt and pepper to taste.

5. Now that the chicken is well-cooked, you can shred it using a fork.

6. Sprinkle avocado slices and cilantro and serve.

Steak tartare is a popular dish. In this recipe we have replaced steak with salmon. In tartare, we use raw salmon, so you need to ensure that the fish is fresh and hygienic. We add some smoked salmon to this dish and some fresh seasoning consisting of herbs, olive oil and red onions, in order to enhance the flavour.

Yield: 4 servings

What you need:

- 14 oz wild salmon fillet cut into chunks

- 7 oz minced, smoked salmon

- 2 Tablespoons minced, pickled cucumber

- 3 Tablespoons minced red onion.

- 1 clove of garlic, minced

- 2 Tablespoons fresh mint, minced

- 2 Tablespoons fresh basil, minced

- Juice of 1 lemon

- 2 Teaspoons dried oregano

- 2 Table spoons Dijon mustard

- 5 Tablespoons extra virgin olive oil

- Sea salt and freshly ground black pepper

How you make it:

1. Take a bowl and add all the ingredients except the salmon and smoked salmon. Mix it well.

2. Add the raw salmon chunks and the smoked salad and mix once again.

3. Add salt and pepper to taste.

4. Garnish it with lime wedges and mint.

5. Serve!

Chicken Soup

Nothing beats a good refreshing soup in the middle of the day. Here is a great recipe for a rich and creamy chicken soup.

Yields: 2 Servings

What you need:

1 cup shredded chicken
1 onion
3 carrots
½ cup mushrooms
Water
1 Teaspoon vinegar
Salt and pepper

How you make it:

1. Finely chop the onion, carrots, and mushrooms.
2. Add in the veggies to a slow cooker. To this add in the shredded chicken.
3. Add water till it covers the chickens and vegetables.
4. Add enough water to fully cover the ingredients.
5. Add the vinegar, salt and pepper and cook till you get the desired consistency.

Yields: 2 Servings
What you need:

2 fish fillets
2 Tablespoons olive oil
1 cup mushrooms
1 onion
1 Teaspoon thyme
1 clove garlic
½ cup parsley
2 Teaspoons arrow root
½ cup water
Salt and pepper

How you make it:

1.   In a pan over medium flame, add in the olive oil and fry the garlic, onions, and mushrooms for 5 minutes.
2.   Add in the thyme, arrow root powder, salt and pepper and keep stirring.
3.   Pre-heat your oven to 180 degrees Celsius.
4.   Add in the water and keep stirring till it thickens. Add in the parsley for a few minutes.
5.   Place the fish in the oven tray lined with the baking paper.
6.   Cover the fillets with mushroom sauce and bake it for around 15-20 minutes.

Chicken with Veggies

Here is a skillet-cooked mix of chicken and veggies with a lively taste.

Yields: 4 Servings

What you need:

1 small chicken
5 onions
1 cup mushrooms
2 Teaspoons vinegar
1 Teaspoon olive oil
1 cup chicken stock
1 bay leaf
2 sprigs thyme
2 oz bacon
¼ cup butter
2 Tablespoons parsley
1 Teaspoon tomato paste

How you make it:

1. Cut the chicken into small pieces.
2. Marinate the chicken with vinegar, thyme and bay leaf for 30 minutes.
3. In a skillet, fry the bacon till it is well cooked. After it is cooked set it aside.
4. Next in the skillet over medium heat, sauté the mushrooms in a little butter for 5 minutes. Remove from flame and set it aside.
5. Next add in little more butter to sauté the onion till it is golden brown. Set it aside.
6. Drain the marinated chicken pieces and keep the remaining marinade in the side. Melt all the remaining butter and throw in the chicken pieces and cook well.
7. Add the remaining marinade, chicken stock and add in the bacon.
8. Next add in the onions and mushrooms.
9. To this add in the tomato paste and cook for 30 minutes.

Tasty Tuna steak with avocado

Tuna has an impressive nutritional profile and this is a perfect way to enjoy fresh tuna. Ginger, lime and cilantro give a refreshing flavour to this dish. Avocado and spinach are rich in nutrients.

Yield: 1 serving

What you need:

- 1 tuna steak
- 3 tablespoons coconut oil
- 1 teaspoon minced ginger
- ½ cup finely chopped cilantro
- 2 cloves minced garlic
- ½ avocado, sliced
- 4 cups of fresh spinach
- Juice and zest of 1 lime
- Sea salt and freshly ground pepper

How you make it:

1. Prepare a marinade with coconut oil, ginger, garlic, cilantro, lime zest and juice, salt and pepper.

2. Marinate the tuna with this mix and wait for 2 hours.

3. Grill the marinated fish in medium heat and allow the tuna to cook on both sides for 4 minutes each.

4. Meanwhile cook the spinach in a skillet for a few minutes.

5. Using the same skillet heat the leftover marinade for a few minutes until it thickens.

6. Take a serving dish and place the spinach in the bottom and the tuna on top.

7. Arrange the avocado slices atop the tuna and add the remaining cilantro marinade to it.

Slow cooked beef and broccoli

Beef and broccoli are equally nutritious. When you combine meat and vegetables, it gives you a complete meal, nutritionally. We add an apple for a special touch, a little bit of sweetness added to the dish. So, here is a power dish that is easy to cook, too.

Yield: 4 servings

What you need:

2-3 cups broccoli florets

1 lb boneless chuck roast, sliced into thin strips
1 thinly sliced apple
1/3 cup of coconut aminos

1/3 cup raw honey

cloves of garlic, minced

How you make it:

1. Mix the beef stock, honey, garlic, apple and coconut aminos in a slow cooker.

2. Add the beef and mix properly. Cook in low heat for 4-5 hours.

3. Add the broccoli and cook for 30 minutes.

Cuban Style Pork Chops

This is a very interesting variation of the traditional pork-fruit combination. We have added more zing to it by adding lime and cumin, and spiced it up with peppercorns. It is served with juicy mango slices that are warmed up a little bit .This is indeed a culinary delight!

Yield: 4 Servings

What you need:

- lb boneless pork loin
- 1 tablespoon cumin seed
- 1 tablespoon freshly cracked black pepper
- cloves of garlic, minced
- 2 tablespoons extra virgin olive oil.
- 2 tablespoons grated lime peel

Ingredients for the mango side dish

- 1 large mango, cut into small slices
- 1 tablespoon raw honey
- Juice from 1 lime
- cloves of garlic, minced
- Cooking fat
- Sea salt and finely ground pepper.

How you make it:

1. Preheat your grill to medium heat.
2. Mix the grated lime, garlic, cumin, olive oil, ground pepper and salt in a bowl to make the Cuban marinade.
3. Marinate the pork chops on both sides.

4. Grill it for 6-8 minutes, turning it ensure that all the chops are cooked well.

Method to prepare the mango side

1. Place a skillet over medium heat and melt the cooking fat in it.

2. Add the garlic and brown it.

3. Add the mango, honey, lime juice and the seasoning.

4. Cook for 4-5 minutes.

Curry Chicken Salad

The cold curry chicken salad is great for lunch.

Yields: 1 Servings

What you need:

2 chicken breasts
1 cup spinach
1 carrot
1 beetroot
1 Tablespoon lemon juice
1 Tablespoon olive oil
1 Teaspoon mustard
1 Tablespoon balsamic vinegar
¼ cup cashews

How you make it:

1. Cut the chicken breast into slices and roast it well in the pan or oven.
2. To this add the spinach, chopped carrots and the chopped beetroots.
3. In a bowl, add in the lemon juice, olive oil, vinegar, and mustard.
4. Add in a few cashews or any other nuts of your choice and stir well.

Sumptuous Salmon with Mushroom

Salmons coupled with creamy mushrooms make one yummy lunch meal.

Yields: 2 Servings

What you need:

4 pieces king salmon steaks
1 cup mushrooms
1 Tablespoon olive oil
½ cup chicken stock
1 Tablespoon garlic
3 Tablespoons butter
½ Tablespoon thyme leaves
2 Tablespoons shallots
1 Tablespoon lemon juice
Salt and Pepper to taste
Parsley leaves

How you make it:

1. Sprinkle olive oil on the salmon fillets. Season it with salt and pepper.
2. In a heavy pan, sauté the mushrooms and keep it aside.
3. Grill the fish till it is well cooked.
4. In the pan add the shallots and garlic and add in the chicken stock. Keep heating till the liquid is half, add in the thyme.
5. In another pan, reheat the mushrooms with butter.
6. Remove the salmon from your grill and top it with the mixture.
7. Garnish with parsley and lemons while serving.

Whole Cauliflower Fried

Yield: 3 serving

What you need:

3 cups of grated raw cauliflowers
2 cups of frozen snow peas
1 cup of carrot, sliced
4 garlic cloves, minced
2 cups of onion, diced
2 tablespoons of olive oil
2 eggs, scrambled with 3 egg whites
2 tablespoons of lemon juice
½ cup of Vegetable stock

How you make it:

1. First, heat oil in the pan and sauté garlic and onions.
2. Once the onions get transparent, add the snow peas and carrots.
3. Add in stock and cook for 10-15 minutes.
4. Once, the vegetables are cooked, stir in the eggs, lemon juice, and cauliflower.
5. Cook for about 10 minutes with the lid on so that steam cooks the ingredients properly.
6. Serve and enjoy.

Lamb Balls with Sauce

Here is a heavenly recipe of lamb meatballs with tomato sauce.

Yields: 2 Servings

What you need:

1 pound lamb
1 egg
2 Teaspoon olive oil
1 Tablespoon oregano
2 Teaspoons sage
2/3 cup tomatoes
1 Teaspoon paprika
1/3 cup basil
1 Teaspoon arrowroot

How you make it:

1. Pre-heat your oven to 180 degrees Celsius.
2. For the lamb balls, in a mixing bowl combine the minced lamb, egg, oregano, and oil. Add in the sage and paprika.
3. Roll into small balls and cook for at least thirthy minutes.
4. For the sauce, dice the tomatoes, add in the basil and salt and cook for 2 minutes.
5. In another cup, mix in the arrowroot powder and a little water. Add this paste into the tomato sauce to make a thick mixture.
6. Serve the meatballs with tomato sauce on the top.

Here is a yummy dessert with no chocolate or carb in it. The rich, creamy coconut filling complements the sweet roasted ambercup squash. The nutmeg and cinnamon add a touch of spice to this dish. It is a healthy dessert and classy and impressive when presented well.

Yield: 2 servings

What you need:
1 ambercup squash

¼ cup raw honey
1 egg white

2 cups of coconut milk

A pinch of nutmeg

2 teaspoon ground cinnamon

How you make it:

1. Remove the seeds of the Squash, after cutting the top off.

2. Place it in a sauce pan and add some water to cover the bottom.

3. Bring the water to a simmer and let it simmer until the flesh of the squash becomes soft.

4. Remove the squash carefully and set it aside.

5. Mix the honey, cinnamon, coconut milk, nutmeg and egg white in a bowl, whipping it until it is mixed well.

6. Get this mixture and pour inside the squash and let it remain for a few minutes until the squash soaks in some of the liquid.

Spiced Roasted Pork

This is deliciously spicy dish that combines the flavors of ginger and cinnamon in roasted pork. Cranberry sauce goes well with all spices and adds its own unique taste to this dish. This can work well as a holiday recipe since all the cooking can be done using an oven proof skillet.

Yield: 4 Servings

What you need:

- lbs boneless pork loin roast
- Sticks of cinnamon
- Cloves
- ½ teaspoon ground nutmeg
- ½ teaspoon ground ginger
- 2 cups chicken stock
- ¼ cup honey
- Cooking fat
- Sea salt and freshly ground pepper

How you make it:

1. Pre heat your oven to 400.
2. Place the skillet over medium heat and add the cooking fat and let it melt.
3. Season the pork with salt and pepper and brown it on all sides in the cooking fat.
4. Add the cloves and cinnamon and cook for 5 more minutes.
5. Turn the roast to ensure consistency.
6. Place the roast in the oven and cook for an hour.

7. Remove the roast and cover with foil.

8. Mix the honey, ginger, nutmeg and stock to form the sauce and bring it to a boil.

9. Lower the heat and let it simmer until the sauce becomes thick.

10. Add salt and pepper to taste.

11. Slice the pork into edible portions and serve with the sauce.

If you are one for curry, here is a fine dish that you will relish. This is a variation of the traditional Indian chicken tikka masala. Fresh cilantro and mint have been added to give it a fresh, citrus flavor. This dish is spicy too since we have added a mix of Indian spices.

Yield: 4 servings

What you need:

- 2 lbs skinless, boneless chicken, cut into 1-inch pieces

- 1 chopped onion

- 1 cup coconut milk

- ½ cup chicken stock

- ½ cup lemon juice

- 2 cups fresh cilantro leaves

- 4 cloves of garlic, minced

- 1 jalapeño pepper, chopped

- 1 cup fresh mint leaves

- 1 ½ teaspoon turmeric

- ½ teaspoon cinnamon

- ½ teaspoon ground cardamom

- 1/8 teaspoon ground cloves

- 3 teaspoons coconut oil

Sea salt and freshly ground pepper to taste

How you make it

1. Heat a skillet over medium heat with the coconut oil and onions.

2. Cook until the onions are soft.

3.   Add the chicken thighs and turmeric and continue cooking for about 7 minutes.

4.   Meanwhile blend the lemon juice, chicken stock, mint, cilantro, jalapeno and garlic in a food processor to form a puree.

5.   After the chicken has cooked for 7 minutes, add the cloves, cardamom and cinnamon and cook for a minute.

6.   Pour in the coconut milk, add the salt, pepper and the herb puree.

7.   Let it simmer for 15 minutes, until the chicken is well cooked

Make delicious chili Paleo style.

Yields: 4 Servings

What you need:

1 pound beef meat
1 cup tomato
4 green chilies
1 onion
1 cup olives
1/2 Tablespoon garlic powder
1 Tablespoons chili powder
1/2 Tablespoon smoked paprika
Salt and pepper, to taste

How you make it:

1. First in a wok, cook the beef pieces till it becomes brown.
2. In another pan, add in the finely chopped tomato, onions and olives and sauté it well.
3. Next add in the chilies and the spices.
4. Finally place the beef pieces in the mixture and cook well.

Your last meal of the day is equally important since you are not going to be eating for a long time. It is pivotal that you make the right choice and ensure a steady supply of nutrients to your body. Here are Tasty and nutritious recipes to keep you going.

This is the perfect dish to warm up with after a long day's work. It is rich and spicy and can be teamed up with spaghetti squash or zucchini noodles. The spices render warmth to this dish and the ghee and coconut milk make it rich and filling.

Yield: 4 servings

What you need:
- 1 lb ground beef

- 1 lb ground pork

- ½ cup almond meal 1 diced onion

- ¼ teaspoon ground allspice

- ¼ teaspoon ground nutmeg

- egg yolks

- 1 cup coconut milk

- cups beef stock

- ¼ cup ghee

- 1 tablespoon tapioca starch

- Cooking fat

- 1 tablespoon chopped parsley leaves

- Sea salt and freshly ground pepper

How you make it:

1. Place a skillet over medium heat and heat the cooking oil until it melts.

2. Add the onions and cook until soft.

3. Mix the pork, beef, egg yolks, almond milk, nutmeg, allspice and cooked onion in a bowl and season it with salt and pepper.

4. Make 1 1/2 inch meat balls with the meat, using clean hands.

5. Add more cooking oil to the skillet and brown the meatballs on all sides and keep it aside.

6. Add ghee to the skillet and melt it on medium heat.

7. Add the beef stock and slowly and cook for 2 minutes, Add the coconut mild and the seasoning of salt and pepper.

8. Remove a small portion of the sauce, add the tapioca starch to it and pour it back into the skillet.

9. Stir continuously and let it thicken.

10. Add the meatballs and cook for 12 to 15 minutes, until it is well-cooked.

11. Garnish with parsley and serve.

Balsamic Roast Beef

This is a magical dish that soaks in the taste and flavor of a rich sauce. The success of this dish lies in the richness of the sauce. This dish requires slow cooking for 8-10 hours. If you do not have a slow cooker, you can cook it in your oven at 200 until the beef turns tender. This recipe makes a full meal which you can have as lunch or dinner.

Yield: 4 Servings

What you need:

·   lb beef chuck roast, boneless

·   carrots cut into big pieces

·   sweet potatoes, cut into big pieces

·   2 sprigs of fresh rosemary

·   1 sliced onion

·   2 bay leaves

·   2 cloves of garlic, minced

·   1/3 cup balsamic vinegar

·   1 cup red wine

·   11/2 cup beef stock

·   2 tablespoons cooking fat

·   Sea salt and freshly ground pepper

How you make it:

1.   Season the roast with salt and pepper.

2. Take a skillet and keep it on medium heat.

3. Add the cooking fat and melt it.

4. Add the roast and sear it for a few minutes on all sides.

5. Place the meat in the slow cooker and add the balsamic vinegar, onions, rosemary springs, bay leaves, beef stock and red wine and cook in low heat for 6 hours.

6. Add the carrots and sweet potatoes and cook on high heat for about 3 hours, until the vegetables and beef are cooked well.

7. Remove the rosemary sprigs and bay leaves.

8. Pour the liquid from the slow cooker into a sauce pan and boil it over medium heat until it is reduced to a desirable consistency.

9. Pour it back into the slow cooker and serve.

Curried Shrimp

Here is a delicious and easy to follow recipe that you can have for dinner.
Yields: 3 Servings

What you need:

2 garlic cloves
4 tomatoes
1 onion
2 Teaspoons ginger
½ Teaspoon cumin
½ Teaspoon coriander
½ Teaspoon turmeric
8 ounces shrimps
2 Teaspoon lemon juice

How you make it:

1.   In a heavy saucepan, heat the olive oil and sauté the garlic and onion until it is tender.
2.   Add in the tomatoes and ginger, cumin, coriander and turmeric.
3.   Simmer it for few minutes.
4.   Place the shrimp in the simmering sauce and cook for 10 minutes until the shrimps are cooked well.
5.   Remove from flame and sprinkle it with lime juice.

Meatballs With Mushroom Sauce

This is one of the great Paleo recipes that easy to make and delicious at the same time.

Yields: 3 Servings

Ingredients Required for Meatballs:

1 pound veal or beef
½ cup mushrooms
½ onion
¼ Teaspoon dried oregano
¼ Teaspoon dried basil
1 egg
2 Tablespoons parsley
1 Teaspoon raw honey
Salt and pepper, to taste

Ingredients Required for Sauce:

1 Tablespoon olive oil
1 Teaspoon thyme
8 ounces mushrooms
¼ cup red wine
1 cup beef broth

How you make it:

1.　In a mixing bowl, add in the chopped onions, eggs, mushrooms and honey. Add in the meat.
2.　Next sprinkle the oregano, parsley, and basil and mix well.
3.　Preheat your oven to 360 Fahrenheit.
4.　Make meatballs which are around 2 inches in size. Place it on a baking sheet. Cook for 30 minutes.
5.　While your meatballs are getting ready, you can start making the sauce.
6.　For the sauce, take a skillet; add in a little olive oil and sauté the mushrooms for 5 minutes over medium heat.
7.　When the meatballs are ready, put them one by one in the sauce. Pour in the beef broth a teaspoon of thyme and allow it to simmer for a few minutes.

8. Pour in the wine and keep stirring till all the flavors have combined.

Crab Stew

Here is a rich and creamy recipe with lots of crab and less of work.
Yields: 3 Servings

What you need:

1 Pound crabmeat
1 cup fish stock
½ cup red wine
2 Tablespoons parsley
3 Tablespoons olive oil
15 Tablespoons tomato paste
4 shallots
1 celery stalk
2 bay leaves
2 Teaspoons thyme
Salt and pepper, to taste

How you make it:

1.   In a bowl, using a fork break the crabmeat and mix it well with the parsley.
2.   In a pan, pour in some olive oil and sauté it over medium heat for 3 minutes.
3.   Pour in the wine and allow it to simmer for 5 minutes.
4.   Next on high heat, pour in the fish stock and tomato paste and keep stirring. Make sure to avoid the formation of any lumps.
5.   Add in the thyme and bay leaves. Keep stirring and allow it to simmer for 15 minutes.
6.   Season it with salt and pepper.
7.   Pour sauce over the crabmeat.

Chili Shrimp

Here is a great recipe for one awesome plate of deliciousness.
Yields: 4 Servings

What you need:

½ cup olive oil
2 cloves garlic
2 pounds shrimp
1 lemon
½ cup chili sauce
2 tomatoes
¼ cup radish
¼ cup parsley

How you make it:

1. In a skillet, pour in the olive oil to sauté the garlic until it turns golden brown.
2. On a higher flame, add in the shrimps to the garlic.
3. When the shrimp turns pink, add in the lemon zest and juice.
4. Next add in the diced tomatoes, chili sauce and chopped radish.
5. Allow it to simmer for a while and then you can remove it from heat. Garnish with parsley.

Here is an aromatic **sea bass** recipe that will leave you smacking your lips.

2 pounds sea bass
3 Tablespoons butter
¼ Teaspoon onion powder
2 cloves garlic, minced
¼ Teaspoon paprika
1 Tablespoon fresh parsley
1½ Tablespoon olive oil
¼ Teaspoon garlic powder
Salt and pepper, to taste

1.   Preheat the grill to high.
2.   In a bowl combine the onion powder, garlic powder, paprika, salt and pepper and mix it well. Rub this mixture all over the fish and set it aside for 10 minutes.
3.   In another bowl, melt the butter.
4.   Grease the grill well and place the sea bass in it. Cook each side for 5-10 minutes.
5.   Drizzle the bass with butter and then flip it and repeat.
6.   Season it well with salt and pepper.

3 Pound Brussels sprouts
1 onion
½ cup butter
¼ cup white vinegar
½ cup pistachios
Salt and pepper, to taste

How you make it:

1. Start by steaming the sprouts till it is tender for about 10 minutes.
2. In a skillet, melt the butter and pour in the vinegar. To this add in the thinly sliced onions and cook it well till it is brown.
3. Add in the steamed sprouts to the skillet and sauté it for 5 minutes. Allow the sprouts to turn golden brown.
4. Season with salt and pepper.
5. Chop the pistachios and add it to the sprouts.

Chicken Kebabs And Eggplant

Easy to prepare, delicious to eat with no compromise in the taste, here's a recipe you will try again and again.

Yields: 2 Servings

What you need for Kebabs:

Skewers
4 chicken pieces
1 onion
1 red pepper
1 green pepper
Olive oil
Salt and pepper to taste

How you make it:

1. In a skillet, pour in the olive oil and over medium heat sauté the onions, green pepper, and red pepper.
2. Add in salt and pepper according to your taste.
3. Dice the chicken pieces
4. Over medium-low heat, place the chicken pieces on the barbeque. Cook it for 10-15 minutes.

What you need for Eggplant:

1 eggplant
2 Tablespoons balsamic vinegar
3 Tablespoons olive oil
2 cloves garlic, minced
Dash of fresh thyme, oregano and basil
Salt and pepper, to taste

How you make it:

1. Slice the eggplants lengthwise in half.
2. In a bowl add the vinegar, olive oil and combine it well.
3. Next mince the garlic, and add thyme, basil and oregano.
4. Brush this mixture on all sides of the eggplant.

5. Place the eggplant over medium-high heat and barbeque it and allow it to cook for 10 minutes on both sides.

Tasty Chicken Lasagna

A rich and classic lasagna Paleo style!

Yields: 2 Servings

What you need:

500g minced chicken
1 onion
1 tomato
3 garlic cloves
2 Tablespoons tomato paste
Dash of sage, basil, thyme, cumin ground
1 Teaspoon cinnamon
1 medium eggplant
2 Tablespoons olive oil
½ cup zucchini
Salt, to taste

How you make it:

1. For the sauce, you need to first sauté the garlic and onion till it is brown. Keep it aside.
2. Next pre-heat your oven to 180 degrees Celsius.
3. Cook the minced meat and keep stirring till they are no big lumps.
4. When the minced meat is well cooked, add in the sautéed onion and garlic into the pan.
5. Next mix in the basil, thyme, sage, salt, and cumin according o your taste.
6. Pour in the tomato paste and cook it for 5 minutes. To this add the diced tomatoes and simmer it for 30 minutes.
7. Slice the eggplant and place it at the bottom of your lasagna dish. Layer it with the mince meat mixture.
8. Add a layer of zucchini slices and any other vegetable you like.
9. Pour another layer of minced meat mixture.
10. Bake it in the oven for 30-40 minutes.
11. Leave it to cool for 10 minutes before serving.

Chicken Satay

This is a scrumptious meat on the stick recipe you are sure to love.
Yields: 2 Servings

What you need:

1 pound chicken breast
1 onion
2 garlic cloves
1 Tablespoon olive oil
¼ cup lemon juice
1 Tablespoon chili flakes
1 Tablespoon ground turmeric
1 Tablespoon ground coriander seeds
1 cup fresh coriander leaves

How you make it:

1.   In a food processor blend the garlic cloves, onions, coriander, olive oil, lemon juice, and turmeric till it forms a smooth texture.
2.   Dice the chicken into little pieces. Marinate the chicken with the mixture and set aside in the refrigerator for a few hours.
3.   Thread the chicken to the skewers and coat it well.
4.   Pre-heat your oven to 180 degrees Celsius.
5.   Place the chicken skewers on a tray. Line it with baking paper.
6.   Bake the chicken in the oven for 30 minutes or until the chicken is cooked well.

This is a nutritious and tasty soup that can take care of your winter sniffle. Kale is a leafy green that is available even during the beginning of winter. Ensure that the carrots and cauliflower that you use are also fresh. The bone broth in the soup makes it appealing to the palate. This soup that can be taken as your main dish along with some vegetables or as an appetizer before your main meal.

Yield: 4 Servings

What you need:
- 1 lb ground turkey
- 4 chopped shallots
- 3 sliced carrots
- 1 bell pepper cut into pieces
- cups chicken stock
- 15 oz can diced tomatoes
- 1 1/2 cup minced cauliflower
- 4 cups kale, ribs removed, leaves cut coarsely
- 2 tablespoons coconut oil

How you make it:
1. Place a sauce pan in medium heat and add the coconut oil.
2. Add carrots, shallot, bell pepper and cauliflower and cook for 8-10 minutes until the vegetables turn soft.

3. Add the turkey and cook for 7-8 min until the meat is fully cooked.

4. Add the chicken stock, diced tomatoes and the seasoning.

5. Bring the soup to a boil. Reduce the heat and add the kale and cover it.

6. Let it simmer for 15 minutes.

Sweet Lemon Shrimp

This is a dish that has an Asian tinge to it and makes easy cooking .Teamed with your favourite vegetable side dish this can be a delicious dinner dish. Or you can serve this as appetizer before a dinner party. It has a sweet tangy taste that is heavenly.

Yield: 4 servings

What you need:

¼ cup coconut aminos

½ cup freshly squeezed lemon juice

1 1/2 lb. shrimp, peeled

Zest of 1 lemon

2 tablespoons honey

½ teaspoon fish sauce

1 clove of garlic, minced

Freshly ground pepper
Sea salt

How you make it:

1. Mix the honey, lemon juice and lemon zest, coconut aminos, fish sauce and garlic in a bowl and add the salt and pepper for seasoning.

2. Marinate the shrimp with this mixture and keep in the refrigerator for a minimum of 30 minutes.

3. Pre heat your oven to 400.Bake the shrimp for 6-8 minutes, until fully cooked.

4. Serve with lime wedges.

Whole 30 Roast Chicken

To roast the chicken, we use red wine. However, red wine contains many anti-oxidants and the alcohol cooks off when the chicken is in the oven. Do not use cooking wine, since it is full of salt.

Yield: 4 servings

What you need:

- 1 whole chicken cut into pieces

- 3 onions, peeled and cut into quarters

- 2 sweet potatoes, peeled and chopped

- 6 carrots peeled and cut vertically

- ¾ cup red wine

- 3 sprigs of thyme, without the leaves

- 4 tablespoons tomato paste

- ¼ cup red wine vinegar

- ½ teaspoon dried marjoram

- Sea salt and freshly ground pepper

How you make it:

1. Take a bowl and mix the tomato paste, red wine, marjoram and red wine vinegar.

2. Season the chicken pieces with salt and pepper.

3. Marinate the chicken with the wine mixture for half an hour or more.

4. Pre- heat your oven to 400.

5. Take a baking dish and add the onions, carrots and sweet potatoes.

6. Arrange the marinated chicken on top of the vegetables.

7. Pour the remaining marinade over the chicken and vegetables.

8. Cover the pan with foil and roast in the oven for 30 minutes.

9. Remove the foil and roast the uncovered chicken for 30-45 minutes.

Tuscan Chicken Skillets

Here is a delicious dish for all those tomato-lovers. It is made more savoury by adding mushrooms and the traditional combination of garlic and herbs. It suits your lifestyle too, since the cooking time is minimal. Chicken tenderloins are extremely lean and cooking them in tomato sauce makes them juicier.

Yield: 4 servings

What you need:

- 1 lb chicken breast tenderloins
- 1 diced onion
- 12 oz sliced mushrooms
- 1 diced onion
- ½ cup sun-dried, chopped tomatoes
- 15 oz fire-roasted diced tomatoes
- ½ teaspoon thyme
- 1 teaspoon oregano
- Cooking fat
- Sea salt and freshly ground pepper

How you make it:

1. Heat a skillet over medium heat and melt to cooking fat in it.

2. Add the chicken and cook each side until it turns brown.

3. Remove the chicken and keep it aside.

4. Add mushrooms into the skillet and cook for a few minutes and set it aside.

5. Add onions and cook it until it becomes soft.

6. Add the garlic and sun-dried tomatoes and sauté it for a few minutes.

7. Add the diced tomatoes, thyme, oregano and the seasoning.

8. Return the chicken into the pan and cover and cook for 10-12 minutes.

9. Add the cooked mushrooms and mix it properly and serve.

Whole Lamb Cutlets

This is a dish with a Mediterranean twist with the lamb, olive oil and olives. The celeriac is a root vegetable that is lighter than potatoes and has a celery flavor. The marinade gives the lamb its flavor and it is easy to cook, too. You can cook up an elegant dinner with this recipe.

Yield: 4 servings

What you need:

- 12 lamb cutlets
- 1 large celeriac
- tablespoons lemon juice
- 1 bunch fresh thyme
- ½ cup extra virgin olive oil
- table spoon fresh chopped parsley
- 2 oz. pitted black olives
- Sea salt and freshly ground pepper

How you make it:

1. Take a container and form a layer with half the thyme.
2. Lay the lamb pieces over it.
3. Marinate the lamb with the remaining thyme, lemon juice and half the olive oil, for at least 2 hours.

4.   Cut the celeriac into medium sized chunks and place it in a pan and add some cold water to it.

5.   Bring the water to a boil, cover and remove from the heat and let it remain for 20 minutes.

6.   Drain the celeriac and return it to the pan.

7.   Add the olives, parsley and the seasoning.

8.   Add the remaining olive oil and stir well.

9.   Take the lamb cutlets out of the marinade and grill it for 2-3 minutes on each side.

10. Serve it on top of the celeriac mix.

Delicious Paleo Spaghetti

In this dish the wheat pasta has been substituted with spaghetti squash which is rich in beta-carotene, potassium and folic acid. The sauce used is Bolognese sauce which is thick and juicy. It is best to use Italian canned tomatoes if you do not have home-grown tomatoes. With this dish, you can enjoy your spaghetti without compromising your health.

Yield: 8 Servings

What you need:

- 1 lb ground grass-fed beef
- tablespoons butter
- ¼ cup chopped bacon
- 1 diced onion
- cloves of garlic, minced
- 2 diced celery sticks
- diced carrots
- 2 teaspoons dried oregano
- 1 tablespoon tomato paste
- 1 bay leaf
- 2 cans of tomato
- Salt and pepper
- Parsley for garnishing

How you make it:

1. Heat a pot and add the cooking fat.

2. Cook the beef and bacon for 5 minutes.

3. Remove the meat and keep it aside.

4. Use the same pot to cook the carrots, celery, onion, garlic and oregano in medium heat, until the vegetables turn soft.

5. Add the bacon, ground beef, tomatoes, bay leaf, and tomato paste.

6. Bring to a boil, after Adding the salt and pepper seasoning. Then simmer it for 45 minutes.

7. At 350 F, Heat your oven to that temperature. Cut the spaghetti squashes in half and remove the seeds.

8. Arrange the halves cut side down in a baking sheet and bake for about 35 minutes.

9. Make sure that they are not overcooked.

10. Cook the Bolognese sauce and add it directly on the squash halves to form bowls.

11. You can add grass fed cheese to the squash and broil it in the oven for 5 minutes, if you choose.

12. Garnish the spaghetti-like pastas with parsley and serve with sauce.

Salmon and Egg Scramble

Yield: 4 servings

What you need:

1 teaspoon of coconut oil
4 organic eggs
3 tablespoons of water
4-6 Oz. small pieces of smoked salmon
2 avocados, sliced
Salt
1 Chopped green onion
Black pepper to taste

How you make it

1. In a large skillet, heat the oil and sauté onion in it.
2. Take a bowl and whisk the eggs with water.
3. Then pour into pan to make an egg scramble.
4. Once the eggs cooked, add in the salmon and stir to make a fluffy omelet.
5. Sprinkle salt and black pepper at the end.
6. Pour the mixture into the plate and serve with the slices of avocado.

Paleo Salmon and Coconut

Yield: 2 Servings

What you need:

2 lbs. of salmon, wild caught
2 teaspoons of coconut oil
Pinch of sea salt and Black pepper, or to taste
6 mint leaves, diced
4 cloves of garlic, peeled, chopped and minced
1 lemon, zest
3 teaspoons lemon juice
2-3 cups of coconut milk
2 tablespoons basil, chopped

How you can make it:

1. Preheat oven at 375 degree F.
2. Place salmon on baking tray and bake in oven for about 15 minutes, until done.
3. Sprinkle salt and pepper over salmon.
4. In a medium frying pan, heat oil and sauté the garlic and add coconut milk.
5. Let it simmer for 5 minutes.
6. Next, add lemon juice, basil, and lemon zest.
7. Pour this mixture over baked salmon.
8. Serve with mint leaves topping.

Mushrooms with Eggs for Breakfast

Yield: 4 servings

What you need:

8 slices of bacon (save drippings)
5 organic eggs, beaten
3 medium onions, finely diced
16 wild mushrooms, finely chopped
Salt and black pepper to taste
4 tomatoes, chopped
3 tablespoons of olive oil

How you make it:

1. In a medium skillet, heat oil and then add onions for Sautéing.
2. Cook for 2 minutes and then add in salt, pepper and tomatoes. Cook for another five minutes.
3. Now add in the mushrooms and bacons.
4. Stir twice and pour the eggs into the mixture.
5. Cook on low heat until the egg gets firm.
6. Serve the delicious omelet as a breakfast.

Egg Drop Soup

Yield: 3-4 Servings

What you need:

4 onions, diced
2 tablespoons of olive oil
16 cups of chicken broth
2 teaspoons of ginger
2 teaspoons of tamari sauce
3 tablespoons water
8 organic eggs
5 stalks of celery
2 tablespoons arrowroot powder

How you make it:

1. Heat oil in a pan and sauté onion and then add celery.
2. Add the chicken broth and ginger as well.
3. Cook until boil come. Then add tamari sauce as well.
4. Meanwhile, in same bowl, mix water with arrowroot powder and add to the cooking pan.
5. Beat eggs in a small bowl and add into the soup, once eggs get fluffy and cooked.
6. The soup is done, serve and enjoy.

Fish and Vegetable Curry

Yield: 2 serving

What you need:

2 lbs. White fish fillets, cut it in a crosswise into 1/2" slices
2 cans unsweetened coconut milk
1 teaspoon of red curry paste
1 small red cabbage, sliced
Handful of cilantro, chopped
Salt and pepper to taste

How you make it:

1. In a large sauté pan, pour the coconut milk and red curry powder.
2. Cook for 5 minutes until the mixture get slightly thicker.
3. Add in the cabbage and let it cook until soften.
4. Add in fish at the end and cook until fish is ready.
5. Sprinkle salt and pepper at the end.
6. Garnish with cilantro and enjoy.

Foods That You Should Stay Away From With the Whole30 Program

Now, that you know all the food that you may eat, you also need to know the food that you should stay away from when you are on the Whole30 program. Here is the food that you should stay away from:

- *Don't eat any things with sugar.*

This is normally the one food that everyone struggles with. You really need to stay away from every food that has added sugar. This means real sugar or even artificial sugar. Samples of these foods are honey, maple, coconut sugar, etc. To be sure of what you are buying, read the labels.

- *Alcohol:*

You really should stay away from any alcohol. And, with this we mean stay away from any form or shape of alcohol, even when the food is cooked with alcohol. And this goes also for any tobacco products also. Alcohol and tobacco products are never good for our bodies, no matter where you are using it.

- *Grains:*

Grains are also not included in the Whole30 plan. You must stay away from any form of grains. This means wheat, rye, barley, rice, buckwheat, etc. This is another reason why you should read your labels. Your food mustn't have any grains as ingredients.

- *Beans:*

Beans are yet another food that you need to stay away from. This includes every kind of beans, from the black beans to peas. And don't even think about peanut butter either. Anything that has beans in should be avoided.

- *Dairy:*

This is also a hard product that you can eat with the Whole30 program. When you can consume dairy, then it includes every single product that has dairy in some form in the product. Here we are talking about milk, cream, cheese, yogurt, etc.

- *Any form of MSG or sulfites:*

If you read your label and it has one of these two ingredients, then you shouldn't even think about buying that food. These ingredients are present in frozen and processed foods. So, be very careful. We don't always look for the MSG or sulfites ingredients on the labels.

Baked foods and junk foods:

Another forbidden food that are hard to leave out. But, this is where most of us go wrong. Don't buy any form of junk food or any baked food. With most of these foods, you are consuming sugar, fat and a lot more ingredients that are not allowed with the Whole30. When you are eating any of the junk food or baked foods then you can just as well leave the whole 30 program. When you cheat on this food, all your work will be for nothing.

How to Succeed With the Whole30 Program

If you really want to succeed with the whole30 program, you need to know these tips and remember it.

· *Plan your means according to your lifestyle.*

It won't do you any good, when you are start planning your program and your meal plans and half way into it, you realize that the meal plans that you have, isn't working for your kind of lifestyle. You need to know what will work with your life and what won't.

· *Make your food look delicious.*

Take the food that you may eat, and what is included in the meal plan and make sure that you are preparing them in such a way that you will still enjoy your food. If you want to succeed, you need to like the foods that you are eating. Otherwise you are going to give up on the program.

· *Take a day, and plan your whole eating plan.*

It isn't a great plan to go day by day and plan as you are going along.

Then you are most definitely going to cheat on the program. Take a day, plan ahead and make sure that you have the correct food available. When you are just eating the things that you have planned, then you will know that you are safe from eating any foods that you are not allowed to eat.

Stay away from dining out.

By going to restaurants, you will find that it is even going to be harder to stay strong and eat only the food that you are allowed to eat. The best is that you should stay away from restaurants altogether and then you don't need to have the temptation of the forbidden and unhealthy foods.

Stay motivated.

This is very important. The moment you are losing your motivation, you are going to give up on the Whole30 program. If you can't stay motivated by yourself, then you should find someone that will be able to motivate you or get a partner that is also doing the same program as you. Then you can motivate each other.

Get your mind in the right place.

You need to stay focused on your diet. Don't let anything or anyone let you lose focus. This can be so easy to "fall of the wagon" when your partner or friends are eating all the things you can't eat while you are on this program.

If you are going to take the whole30 program challenge of 30 days, you need to know on how you can achieve the maximum weight loss with this program. Here are some points to know.

· The first thing that you should do when you start on your whole30 program is that you should go through your kitchen cabins, and throw out all the products and foods that aren't allowed in this diet. When you don't have the foods, you can't eat these foods.

· You still need to exercise in some way. Even, if you are on the whole30 program that is a great program with a lot of success stories, you still need to get in shape by exercising frequently. When you are exercising, you will lose weight and become fit and healthy even faster. Exercise is always important, no matter on what program you are on.

· Don't even think about cheating even once on this program. When you are cheating on this program, you are cheating on yourself and you don't teach your body not to crave all the unhealthy foods that you are trying not to eat.

Conclusion

To be able to achieve maximum weight loss, you need to know that this is going to take some time to get used to and that it is going to take a lot of effort in making sure that you are eating the right foods. But, you will be glad about the results of the Whole30 program.

It can be tough to stay on the Whole30, but just remember that the reward is going to be even greater. There isn't anything better in life than a healthy and fit body. With the right motivation and guidance, the Whole30 program will be also beneficial for you, just like the hundred others that have tried the diet and succeed.

Thank You

If you follow religiously to The Whole 30: It Starts With Food And some of the Mouthwatering and healthy recipes outlined in this book. You are going to be seeing great results in your body and health in just 30 days, because it is proven to work.

If you enjoyed the recipes in this book, please take the time to share your thoughts and post a positive review with 5 star rating on Amazon, it would encourage me and make me serve you better. It'd be greatly appreciated!

Other Recommended Health & Fitness Books

It Starts With Food: Discover the Whole30 and Change Your Life in Unexpected Ways, By Dallas & Melissa Hartwig

Get it Here>> http://amzn.to/1NZzrUv

Spiralized Cookbook: 50 All-New Delicious & Healthy Veggetti Spiral Recipes to Help You Lose Weight, Lower Blood Pressure

Using Vegetable Pasta Spiralizer- for Paderno, Veggetti Shredders!

Get It Here>> http://amzn.to/1zKYCk7

10-Day Detox Diet Cookbook: 50 All-New Recipes to Help you Burn the Fat, Lose weight Fast and Boost your Metabolism For Busy Mom By Laura Hill

Get It Here>> http://amzn.to/1MxCP04

10-Day Green Smoothie Cleanse: 35 Yummy Green Smoothies Recipes to Help Lose 15lbs in 10 Days!

Get it Here>> http://www.amazon.com/10-Day-Green-Smoothie-Cleanse-Smoothies-ebook/dp/B00U1U3JTS

My food Babe Diet Recipes: 37 Delicious & Healthy Recipes to help you lose weight in 21 Days. The Food Babe Way!

Get it Here>> http://www.amazon.com/food-Babe-Diet-Recipes-Delicious-ebook/dp/B00UNCNUX4

CPSIA information can be obtained at www.ICGtesting.com
Printed in the USA
LVOW04s0244180815

450551LV00030B/842/P